NEIGHBORHOOD:
A STATE OF MIND

Pat —
"Happy Birthday" '01
Enjoy!
Love,
Carol and Jay

D0998900

NEIGHBORHOOD
A STATE OF MIND

Linda G. Rich

Joan Clark Netherwood and Elinor B. Cahn

Photographs and Interviews
from the East Baltimore Documentary
Photography Project

FOREWORD BY WRIGHT MORRIS

Introduction by David T. Lewis
and David J. Boehlke

The Johns Hopkins University Press

Baltimore and London

Publication of this book has been made possible
in part by grants from Sandra and George Dalsheimer;
the National Endowment for the Arts; the Maryland Committee
for the Humanities, through a grant from the National Endowment
for the Humanities, Office of State Programs; C & P Telephone
Company of Maryland; Union Trust Company of Maryland; the
H. Barksdale Brown Charitable Trust; the Noxell Foundation, Inc.;
U.S.F.&G. Foundation, Inc.; and Baltimore Gas
& Electric Company.

The Johns Hopkins University Press, Baltimore, Maryland 21218
The Johns Hopkins Press Ltd., London

Originally published (hardcover and paperback), 1981
Second printing (paperback), 1982

Library of Congress Cataloging in Publication Data

Rich, Linda G.
Neighborhood.

1. East Baltimore (Baltimore, Md.)—Social life
and customs. 2. East Baltimore (Baltimore, Md.)—
Description. 3. Baltimore (Md.)—Social life
and customs. 4. Baltimore (Md.)—Description.
I. Netherwood, Joan C. II. Cahn, Elinor B.
III. Title.
F189.B16E376   975.2'6   81-5992
ISBN 0-8018-2558-X   AACR2
ISBN 0-8018-2559-8   pbk

CONTENTS

FOREWORD

This innovative study of East Baltimore neighborhoods would have found a close and appreciative reader in Gertrude Stein, once a resident of the city and author of a portrait of three Baltimore women whose descendants might well have participated in this project. Stein was one of the first and most profound students of what is uncommon in the commonplace. Readers of her work soon share her perception that there are no ordinary people. Very ordinary thinking and customs we have, and will always have, but we are each intricately and cunningly made, and ineffably individual. From that virtue, alas, derive many problems. What conceivable social order will long contain so many conflicting forces? One of the most durable is so commonplace that we ignore it. The *neighborhood* is the organic response to this need, and in East Baltimore it commingles the traditions of the parish with the pressing needs of modern urban life. This book is the portrait of one that has gathered its forces in an act of renewal and survival.

To understand the true nature of this effort we must acknowledge the obstacles. Deep and gratifying ethnic differences, and suspicions, have resulted in carefully guarded privacies, in the public sociability of the tavern, the marble stoop, and the summer sidewalk. These confinements understandably generate outbursts of public and private feeling, some of which are channeled into patriotic fervor. The proximity of house against house, yard fencing yard, window confronting window, is both comforting and claustrophobic. This is a *living* organism we are concerned with, and it feels different from hour to hour, from day to day, just as we do. The complexity of the resulting *state of mind* is profoundly revealed in the photographs, but many of these revelations are coded and require a lifetime of sympathetic consideration.

With its profound need to both nurture and sustain, the neighborhood is a very womanly organism, and it is women who administer to its survival. They are present concretely in the photographs and in the fragments of old wives' tales we lend an ear to in the oral texts. I find it appropriate that Linda Rich, Joan Netherwood, and Elinor Cahn are responsible for the exceptional photographs. I doubt that a man would have won the confidence of the residents or gained access to what they have so craftily guarded. The photographs sometimes approximate the view that the subjects have of themselves, and would have taken had they been able. The skill and sympathy this requires are great, and are available only to those who understand and respect both the camera's eye and that of the subject. No method or formula is useful in approaching people who are not accustomed to public inquiry or exposure. Their trust is won by becoming a neighbor, like themselves.

The photographers were first drawn to this world by their interest in what constituted a viable neighborhood, but they were held to it, over several years, by growing ties of affection and understanding. In this awareness and cultivation of a shared human condition we have the clue to survival that so many urban neighborhoods seem to be lacking.

The central and dynamic tension of American life, at once challenging and thwarting, is that between established traditional values, time-honored customs, and a culture inflexibly committed to change. East Baltimore provides a laboratory model for these durable conflicts, but it is exceptional in the manner in which it now attempts to resolve them. The recognition that the young, for all their new ideas and strange customs, are the ones who stand up and fight "city hall" in a way that the elders would never dream of has provided both age groups with the ingredients that will soon make them all good neighbors. The neighborhood itself is a living tissue, a vibrant web that both snares and entangles, and the presence of the web can be felt in both cherished and confining traditions, and in the oral comments of residents where private concerns are made public: "Well, it's changing, but everything is changing...so what are you going to do?"

How the world was made often filled Gertrude Stein's "Melanctha" with despair, as it will most of those who try to comprehend it. But a neighborhood is more to our human scale. I am not a scholar of this genre of social commentary but I have found the texts and photographs of this study informative, revealing, and above all life-enhancing. The poet Auden somewhere made this observation: "We are all on earth to help each other, but what the others are here for, God only knows."

One of the things we are here for finds its culmination in these Baltimore neighborhoods, where human frailties are fully acknowledged and human relationships sustained and fostered. I commend all those who gave themselves to this project, and The Johns Hopkins University Press for this handsome production.

Wright Morris

PREFACE

In 1975 I moved to Maryland to accept a teaching position at the Maryland Institute, College of Art, in Baltimore. On one of my first excursions in Baltimore I was taken to view the "I Am an American Day" parade, East Baltimore's annual tribute to patriotism and politics. As I chased marching band after marching band through many of East Baltimore's neighborhoods, I passed long blocks of pristinely maintained row houses. I was fascinated by the white marble steps that adorn the front entrances, the scenic, painted window screens, and the lace-curtained front windows, which are individualized by the presence of religious icons, American flags, greeting cards, and flower arrangements—clues to the lives of the people who live inside. Never before had I encountered an urban community so densely built upon. Yet it appeared so livable, so inviting. The valued traditions of its people were evident everywhere: pride in homeownership, close family ties, hard work, and religious devotion. These people and their neighborhoods continued to be a part of my thoughts long after the day of the parade.

It wasn't until I was teaching a course in social documentary photography a year later that these impressions began to be molded into what became the East Baltimore Documentary Photography Project. Joan C. Netherwood and Elinor B. Cahn were students in that class. As a class project, the three of us decided to make a portrait of the neighborhoods of East Baltimore. Our intent was to photograph the people, to enter their lives, and to see them as they see themselves.

We began by contacting the clergy at a few of the nearly one hundred churches in East Baltimore. In a community with such a strong religious identity, an introduction by a neighborhood religious leader meant easier acceptance of us by the parishioners. Gradually we began to be invited to bingo luncheons, exercise classes, holiday parties, graduation ceremonies, first communions, sauerbraten suppers, and neighborhood tours. We attended as many meetings of community associations and met as many community leaders as possible. We patronized local shops and markets, describing our project and asking to make photographs. During the semester we realized that we had discovered a very special quality of life in East Baltimore. When the course ended we chose to continue the project independent of the classroom. Our lives and the project merged.

Through months of observing, talking, interviewing,* and photographing, our concept of the project broadened into an exploration of what constitutes a neighborhood, not as a geographical but as a moral and social concept. There would be images of buildings and places, but our emphasis would be on the people: at home, on the street, at work, in the bars, celebrating holidays, in church, at play, getting married, christening their newborn, and burying their dead.

To keep our East Baltimore neighbors abreast of our progress, we gave photographs to our subjects and mounted many "in progress" exhibitions. We arranged to show a selection of our photographs at seven East Baltimore churches, keying the exhibitions to church events and the pictures to the people of the particular parish. These church exhibits were

---

*The quotations that accompany each section of photographs in this book have been taken from individually taped interviews with both past and present residents of East Baltimore.

so warmly received that neighbors "borrowed" photographs, returning them after proudly showing them to friends and family.

We also sponsored four formal exhibitions and concurrent lecture programs. The exhibits included historic photographs of East Baltimore, excerpts from the taped interviews, and our own photographs. Many of our finest historic photographs came from the family archives of the people we were photographing. The lecture programs provided an overview of the scope of documentary photography. The purpose of the exhibitions and lectures was to relate our photographs to the history, culture, and social concerns of East Baltimore and to create for the residents a clearer sense of the richness of their lives.

We were most gratified when hundreds of East Baltimoreans, photography enthusiasts, and members of the greater community came to see each exhibit and hear the lecture programs. East Baltimoreans further participated in these events by preparing home-baked ethnic specialties for the opening receptions. Neighbors stood by photographs of themselves, proudly bringing them to life—a clear sign that our project had become a meaningful one in the community.

We owe the success of this project to good fortune, good timing, hard work, many volunteers, and generous financial support. Its completion is a testimonial to the power of positive thinking. We are honored that the residents of East Baltimore so openly and warmly have shared their lives with us. This book is dedicated to them.

Linda G. Rich
Project Director

ACKNOWLEDGMENTS

We would like to acknowledge the contributions of the many individuals and organizations that have made the East Baltimore Documentary Photography Project and this book possible. For their assistance in the initial stages of the project and for generously sharing their time throughout, we would like to thank our planning committee: Richard P. Davis, Michael Franch, Suzanne Greene, Barbara Hoff, Kenneth Kahn, Father Ed Kenney, and Matilda Koval. We are especially grateful to David Lewis, David Boehlke, and Jacqueline Lampell for their wholehearted dedication to and energetic efforts on behalf of the project, invaluable guidance at every stage, and moral support.

We would like to express our appreciation for its overall support to the Maryland Institute, College of Art, our sponsoring organization.

Generous financial support for the research, the photography, the interviews, the exhibitions, the lecture programs, the slide archive, and the preparation of this book has been provided by American National Building and Loan Association; Art Seminar Group, Inc.; William G. Baker, Jr., Memorial Fund; Mrs. David A. Breitstein; Mrs. Nora W. Dorf; Eisenberg Educational Foundation; The Equitable Trust Company; Mr. and Mrs. Peter Frenchy; Mr. and Mrs. Herbert D. Hammond; Matilda and Joe Koval; The Dr. Frank C. Marino Foundation, Inc.; Maryland Arts Council; Maryland Committee for the Humanities; Mayor's Advisory Committee on Art and Culture; Mayor's Office of Manpower Resources, C.E.T.A. Program; National Endowment for the Arts; National Endowment for the Humanities; Lt. Col. (Rt'd) and Mrs. George M. Riser; Alice and Eugene H. Schreiber; and Mrs. Jack Wasserman.

We thank the following collectors and organizations for purchasing our photographs and limited edition portfolios: Academy of the Arts, Easton, Maryland; C&P Telephone Company of Maryland; Mary Pat Clarke; Steve Crumlin; Design Form, Inc.; East Baltimore Neighborhood Housing Services, Inc.; Nanette and Irvin Greif, Jr.; Lisa Kaslow; Mr. and Mrs. Robert Keller; Library of Congress; Maryland Institute, College of Art; National Artists' Alliance, Inc.; National Commission on Neighborhoods; Lt. Col. (Rt'd) and Mrs. George M. Riser; Dolores Soul; Southeast Land Bank; Staples and Charles; and the University of Maryland Baltimore County. Photographs were purchased for publication by American Planning Association; Department of Housing and Urban Development; Ridge Press, Inc.; Time-Life Books, Inc.; and the Urban Reinvestment Corporation. The funds raised from these purchases enabled us to continue to buy photographic supplies and subsidize this book.

We thank the following organizations for supplying various materials and special services: Agfa Gevaert, Inc.; Baltimore-Warner Paper Co.; the City of Baltimore; Garamond/Pridemark Press; Ruth and Morris Garbis; Hollinger Corporation; Reico; Norman Rukert, Southeast Land Bank; and Ed Wladkowski.

We owe unending appreciation to Ruth Garbis, who so generously contributed her time and so diligently assisted us with secretarial work, interviewing, transcribing interview tapes, and many other details too numerous to mention.

Many Baltimore neighborhood organizations provided invaluable suggestions and continuous cooperation, particularly Neighborhood Housing Services, Inc.; the Southeast Community Organization; and Citizens Planning and Housing Association. Hundreds of East Baltimoreans furnished information and insights into their neighborhoods; unfortunately, it is not possible to name them here.

We thank Mayor William Donald Schaefer and the city of Baltimore for their overall support. Within the mayor's office we are grateful to Margaret Daiss, curator of City Hall, and to the Art Commission of Baltimore City, for the sponsorship of two of our major Baltimore exhibitions. We thank the entire staff of the Baltimore Museum of Art, especially Robert Zimmerman, Melanie Harwood, Dan Sellers, and Anthony Boening, for their creativity and hard work in installing our exhibitions.

For loaning the project historic photographs of East Baltimore for use in the exhibitions we thank the Baltimore *News American,* the Baltimore *Sunpapers,* the Maryland Historical Society, the Library of Congress, the University of Maryland Baltimore County, the Peale Museum, the National Museum of History and Technology of the Smithsonian Institution, and many residents of East Baltimore.

For their participation in the lecture programs and photographic criticism we owe special appreciation to Professor Cavalliere Ketchum, the University of Wisconsin; Professor Jerome Liebling, Hampshire College; Professor Walter Rosenblum; Brooklyn College; and Jack Wilgus, Maryland Institute, College of Art.

For administrative assistance we thank Lyn Kargaard, Mary Pat Tucker, and Nancy Wicks.

For their help at various times and in most valuable ways, we thank Joe Arnold, Virginia Cassiano, Patti Cass, Michael Harris, Quentin Moseley, Kimberly Paisley, Frank Wheat, and Beverly Wilgus.

Our thanks go to those people in the photographic community who gave helpful criticism and warm support throughout the project.

Finally, we owe our deepest gratitude to our husbands, George P. Jadowski, Paul H. Netherwood, Jr., and Charles M. Cahn, Jr., whose contributions have perhaps been the most subtle of all.

The photographic archive upon which this book is based is placed at the Peale Museum, the municipal museum of Baltimore; the Visual Resource Center of the Maryland Arts Council; and the National Endowment for the Arts.

INTRODUCTION

Baltimore, Maryland, has been called a "Cinderella city." It has become an acknowledged leader in redeveloping its existing housing stock through a responsive political structure and the active daily involvement of its citizens. A prominent sector in this resurgence has been East Baltimore, nationally acclaimed as a model for ethnic neighborhood revitalization.

A PRACTICAL DESIGN

East Baltimore has thrived as a distinct and defined area of the city of Baltimore for over 150 years, with between fourteen and seventeen neighborhoods (depending on how the boundaries are drawn) that vary in area, size of population, and length of history. Fells Point is the oldest, predating the existence of Baltimore City itself, while some neighborhoods have come into their own only in the last few years. The total population of East Baltimore stands near 75,000, with individual neighborhoods varying from 1,000 to slightly over 10,000 residents and ranging in size from 12 to 128 square blocks.

East Baltimore was laid out before the streetcar and the automobile altered the face of American cities. Some neighborhoods, built just after the Civil War, were planned developments that included housing, retail, and industrial sites, all within easy walking distance of each other. With a few exceptions, the neighborhoods conform to a predictable urban grid. The east-west streets boast forty-foot-wide spans and broad sidewalks; the north-south streets are alternately wide and narrow, and range from ten to forty feet in width. The width of the street was very significant to the neighborhood layout, as it determined the size of the houses. Houses on

the broadest streets are relatively wide and tall, giving prominence to their more elegant location. These three-story houses with impressive high-ceilinged rooms were built on raised basements, and many are twenty feet wide and sixty feet deep. The houses on the narrower streets are more modest: two stories tall, they were built directly on the ground, and often are only ten feet wide and twenty feet deep. Regardless of their size, both types of houses conform to the same architectural pattern: the row house. Each city block projects a continuous face of up to twenty-five houses on each side of the street. With the exception of but a dozen structures, the twenty thousand houses are brick. When the rows were built, the corner buildings were designed to accommodate stores, taverns, or offices. Only the first-floor front distinguishes these commercial units from the rest of the block.

THE PEOPLE: SHARED VALUES

When immigrants from southern and eastern Europe arrived in the United States between 1880 and 1921, many settled into houses in East Baltimore that were vacated as earlier American, Irish, and German residents moved out of the central city. These new immigrants came from Lithuania, Russia, Hungary, Poland, Greece, Italy, and the Ukraine. They brought with them the Roman and Eastern Orthodox Catholic traditions that are still upheld by their descendants in East Baltimore. Despite their separate cultural histories, most of the residents of East Baltimore today share a European background and, for the most part, a common religious identification.

Over the years, the make-up of the population has changed a bit, but the influx of newcomers has never threatened the strong

social norms established by the original southern and eastern Europeans. There had always
been pockets of black people in East Baltimore,
but during World War II the growth of steel
production and shipbuilding attracted more
blacks, some Lumbee Indians from North and
South Carolina, and Appalachian whites, who
could afford housing only in the poorer fringe
areas. More recently, some newcomers, largely
people from other city neighborhoods and the
older suburbs, have moved into the community and rehabilitated some of the vintage
housing. These newer residents have generally
been well accepted because they respect many
of the values of their older neighbors: love of
country, strong religious devotion, dedication
to hard work, and pride of ownership.

For the past thirty years East Baltimoreans
have vividly demonstrated their love for their
country by hosting and participating in the "I
Am an American Day" parade, a spectacle that
may take up to four hours to pass a given spot.
Along the parade route viewers take seats on
the stoops early or line up chairs along the
sidewalk. Curbs fill with crowds and American
flags fly from second-floor windows. Neighbors chat with each other, children shout and
play, and vendors peddle their wares. Police
have estimated recent crowds at three hundred
thousand, although the community numbers
only one-quarter of that. Whenever the American flag passes, people pay it respect with
salutes, hands over hearts, and hats off. Decorated floats, military units, fire companies,
antique cars, past and present beauty queens,
drum and bugle corps, majorette units, Boy
Scout and Girl Scout troops, mounted police,
dozens of bands, as well as decorated sanita-
tion vehicles and uniquely Baltimorean
"Arabers" (vendors selling fruits and vegeta-

bles from horse-drawn wagons) all participate.
Politicians from all levels of government are
on hand to mingle with the crowds, shake
hands, and kiss babies.

Patriotism fills the homes of East Baltimoreans, too: photographs of men in uniform are
prominently displayed. The neighborhood
bars proudly exhibit military photographs of
the owner and relatives, along with American
flags draped over the mirror behind the bar.
The Pledge of Allegiance opens most meetings,
from veterans' clubs to parish councils. And
during the last years of the Vietnam War, no
one burned draft cards or marched in defiance
of the war. Chances are, if the government
reinstated the draft today, the citizens of East
Baltimore would support it, because, to them,
loyalty to their country is as strong as their
belief in God. Neither is questioned.

Religion plays an integral role in the lives of
East Baltimoreans. East Baltimoreans express
their religious devotion by decorating their
homes with religious icons. Statues and
figurines often line windowsills and are
placed side by side with potted rosebushes
in many backyards. Although there are active
Protestant congregations, the community is
still predominantly Catholic. Many activities
center around the churches, including chris-
tenings, weddings, funerals, and bazaars with
ethnic foods and handicrafts for sale. These
organized events not only provide an oppor-
tunity for neighbors to gather and visit, but out
of them emerge the community leaders who
work to preserve the values that neighbors
share.

The residents of East Baltimore have adapted
their lives to the structure of the neighborhoods. The older neighborhoods were originally planned so that everyone could walk to

work—and many people still do. A number of industries still remain there, and the value of a house does not decrease just because it may be near factories. In fact, the clatter of metal stamping or an occasional pungent belch from a chemical plant assures the residents that jobs still exist for them. The factories, and the cafes, bars, and union halls that surround them, give the neighbors not only a place to work, but also a friendly environment in which to live.

Blue collar workers make up a good part of the community. For most, the day starts early, at the meat-packing plant, the steel mill, or the automobile assembly line. Some, particularly women, work in the hospitals or wait on tables. Others work as house painters, roofers, or asphalt pavers, or as carpenters, siding and window installers, or masons. The trades most workers aspire to are the cleaner ones: locksmith, crane operator, mail carrier, or shop steward. A few of the residents become priests, ministers, teachers, or social workers, and there is a sprinkling of doctors and lawyers.

For most of the workers in the major plants in the area, job layoffs are not uncommon. During such times, relatives pitch in with loans of fifty or one hundred dollars. Often a father will lend money to his son, expecting him to pay it back when he can. Nowadays, though, it is becoming hard to help out, especially for retired people. Therefore, small loan offices have moved into the community to help the residents make it through the difficult times. East Baltimoreans have accepted the loan companies into their neighborhoods and do not see them as exploitative corporations. For many, the loan company is a necessity and a steadfast friend, who conducts business on a first name basis, just as the corner grocery store does. As soon as the borrowers return to work, they begin to pay off their loans, knowing that they will probably be back at the loan company before long. During a layoff, neighbors often pitch in with bags of groceries, but only after a few weeks have passed; it is assumed that each family has stored enough extra groceries to weather an emergency. Local grocery stores may help by extending credit to their regular customers, another example of the mutual trust that today exists mainly in small towns.

PRIVATE LIVES, PUBLIC PLACES

East Baltimoreans draw a sharp line between the private interiors and the public exteriors of their row houses. Hand-painted screens installed on the windows and front doors of many homes symbolize this insistence on privacy. These screens serve the purpose of one-way glass, as occupants can look out but people passing by cannot look in. Many of the front windows have wooden shutters, curtains, and blinds drawn halfway down. One story has it that when an owner was renovating his house to rent it, he replaced the front door with a copy of the original that had a clear glass transom. When the owner stopped by to see his tenant a few days later, he found that she had covered the transom with paper, even though it was high enough that no one could possibly see in. The glass let in outside light, and that was reason enough to cover it.

Often the inside windowsills hold decorations depicting the season or the current holiday. Some decorations, especially figurines and vases, are on view for months at a time. The windows may announce special events: "Welcome home, Billy" or "It's a girl! Seven pounds, five ounces." They also serve as billboards, displaying notices of church suppers or neighborhood meetings.

East Baltimoreans demand privacy inside their homes and follow definite social rules about who may visit. Only close family members may stop in. Even nextdoor neighbors, regardless of how friendly they may be, do not casually drop by.

The faces of the houses are meticulously cleaned and maintained, just as the interiors are. Because the older, less expensive houses were built of unglazed red bricks that allowed moisture to penetrate the walls, the bricks must be painted regularly: The mortar between the bricks is often "striped" with thin lines of heavy white enamel, boldly outlining the painted bricks. This painting is functional, not simply an extension of the desire for neatness. In recent years, Formstone, a maintenance-free, cementlike plaster used to cover the face of a block of row houses, has served this practical purpose, while at the same time its quarry stone appearance pleases the residents who came from areas in Europe where stone is a familiar building material.

The windows of the homes are scrupulously maintained. Every spring and fall, and for certain holidays, the residents wash their windows. Until recently, the shades were changed to complement the season—blue for summer and white for winter.

East Baltimoreans do not have backyards large enough to play or rest in. Most yards consist of paved areas ten feet wide and twenty feet deep, surrounded by a cement or cinder block wall five feet six inches high. The wall is high enough for some privacy but low enough to allow city inspectors to see the yard. Few residents plant gardens; they prefer to grow flowers or vegetables in pots, and fill their backyards with wading pools for the children and lines of freshly washed clothes. Neighbors rarely barbeque, picnic, or visit in their backyards except on occasions such as the Fourth of July, when families along a block may celebrate, each in its own yard.

East Baltimoreans consider the stoop and front sidewalk to be a part of their house, and they keep them just as tidy. The cleanliness and lack of litter impresses many visitors, especially in view of the large number of people living in such close proximity. It is not uncommon to see women on their knees vigorously scrubbing their steps, while the men often hose down the sidewalk. People accustomed to living on tree-lined streets find the absence of trees in East Baltimore austere and rather unpleasant. For East Baltimore residents, however, the lack of trees is a deliberate choice, and they have successfully prevented the city from planting many. If asked why, the neighbors quickly and firmly respond, "Trees! Trees bring birds and birds drop on our cars." "When you've got trees, you've got bathrooms for dogs." "They shade the steps on cool mornings when you want some warmth." "Trees mean leaves, and that means more cleaning up." Beauty is in the eye of the beholder, and in this area, that means wide, clean streets with open vistas and uniform, well-maintained houses.

In East Baltimore there are very few front porches or front yards. On nearly every house the front steps rest on the public sidewalk. Most of the front steps are constructed of marble, although some are made of brick or concrete. Since most of the row houses are narrow, each stoop is about ten feet from the next. That is close enough for conversation with nextdoor neighbors, but far enough for those who want only to pass the time of day. Usually people are content to carry on conversations with neighbors from their own front stoop, but occasionally someone who has a choice bit of gossip will move to a neighbor's stoop. People often sit on the stoop after work and drink beer or wine while dinner is cooking. Retired people spend their afternoons chatting there. For adults the stoop is an extension of the living room; for teens, a courting area; and for children, a play area. From its stoop, a family can see everyone and learn everything that is happening on the block from early in the morning to dark. The stoops, the sidewalks, and the streets of East Baltimore are where neighbors socialize, discuss problems, and plan activities to protect their neighborhoods. They are essential points of communication, tying people together within blocks, linking blocks to neighborhoods, and joining neighborhoods to the greater community.

FACING THE CHALLENGES

After World War II, East Baltimore suffered from many of the disruptive changes that affected major cities across the country. Lending companies began investing their money in suburban development rather than in the cities. Employment at the nearby docks declined as the new, larger ships had to use docks farther down the Chesapeake Bay. The residents saw a gradual decline in services and an increase in crime. The community began to show signs of wear, both physical and social. Many homes were vacated as elderly residents died and young ones married and moved to other communities. What started as a slow deterioration of the neighborhoods grew rapidly into a major problem of absentee landlords; boarded-up, rat-infested houses; vandalism; and declining corner businesses. At the same

time, traffic increased, bringing countless heavily loaded tractor-trailers through the neighborhoods. Buildings shook, front walls cracked, roads began to break up, and diesel exhaust filled the air. The streets, so important to the way people had organized their lives, had become dangerous.

THE RESPONSE

Often urban communities have been unable to stop this kind of decline and deterioration; many original residents abandon the area, leaving behind the oldest homeowners and the incoming poor and minorities. But East Baltimore proved different. Even though the residents were apprehensive about the changes, and at first felt powerless to control their neighborhoods, they began to organize and dramatically show the effectiveness of people working together. They sought out both the culprits of decline and the potential partners in reasserting control over their future. Literally hundreds of East Baltimoreans took to the streets with brooms. One day they formed a human barrier to truck traffic on their blocks. They fought for the return of such basic city services as adequate trash removal, street cleaning, and public health care. They knew, however, that the problems required more complex solutions than just increases in public services. They made countless personal decisions, small but essential, which demonstrated their dedication to rebuilding their neighborhoods. They continued shopping at the corner stores, kept their children in the integrated public schools, and walked to the same churches they had always attended.

When the city of Baltimore proposed a major highway system that would cut through many East Baltimore neighborhoods and require demolition of buildings in its path, the community organized to fight for the preservation of their homes. The Southeast Community Organization (SECO) was formed to embody and act upon their concern. SECO played a major role in stopping the highway from going through the community and also has protected the community from being part of certain unwise urban renewal projects.

Gradually SECO moved from fighting undesirable change to promoting changes it considered to be in the best interest of the community. Neighbors wanted to do more than fight city hall. They wanted to play a creative role, to help shape the future of their neighborhoods. But while fighting unwanted changes had required strong organization but little money, initiating positive changes requires not only organization but also a great deal of money and a healthy, cooperative relationship with city hall. A year after its formation, SECO was able to qualify for federal and city funds. The money was used to hire a staff and launch a number of programs.

An organization called Neighborhood Housing Services was one of the first and most important initiated by SECO. Formed as a nonprofit partnership of residents, lenders, and city officials, the association quickly gained fame for its block-by-block approach to neighborhood revitalization. Again, the neighbors set the pattern for the organization. The already hard-pressed, often elderly, homeowners were unwilling to improve their homes significantly unless the worst of the vacant and absentee-owned homes were also improved. To accomplish this, new homeowners bought vacant houses and many tenants were able to purchase their homes from their landlords, often with the assistance of special city and private lending programs. Neighborhood groups backed by SECO persuaded the city to rehabilitate several blocks of houses instead of constructing garden apartments, whose architecture would contrast dramatically with that of the outward-facing row houses. The houses were rehabilitated as cooperative apartments, owned and managed by the residents.

Additional organizations have greatly helped the revitalization of East Baltimore. One agency seeks out new industry and better retailing in the commercial district: concerned neighbors formed a community-based revitalization corporation to carry out promotional campaigns and inject new confidence when businesses began to close. In another case, a neighborhood wanted its own supermarket, so one organization became the prime sponsor and partial owner of a new store. Other, large groups have gathered to fight problems that may affect only a small number of people. For example, flooding was a problem for only a few blocks of houses, yet the larger community supported the plea for a new sewer. A prison was to be built near forty houses, yet busloads of people from throughout East Baltimore showed up for the hearings at the state capital.

When moderate-income renters saw their housing opportunities decreasing, they organized and then aired their grievances in the press, and, at the same time, solicited funds to form a corporation to buy, rehabilitate, and rent quality housing.

Not all of the efforts have been so grand. Much of the work is mundane and repetitious, carried out at monthly meetings where city officials bring the residents up to date on the number of new curbs installed or the two-year process to get one vacant house rehabilitated. Many times the fight is simply to see that an alley stays clean. One housewife was so incensed when trashbags were put out for collection on the wrong days that she would pick through the garbage, looking for an old envelope or a medicine prescription bottle that could identify the culprit. She would then rebundle the garbage and return it to its owner. Another neighbor stayed a step ahead of the city inspector by checking the exterior of every house in his neighborhood and giving negligent owners a list of potential violations before the city inspector ever visited. He and others later founded a low-cost program to help homeowners repair their houses.

The people of East Baltimore continue to face challenges that test their strength and determination. But they have a history of commitment to one another, and they look toward the future with optimism. The photographs in this book were taken as the community's fortunes were turning upward, and they reveal a sense of security as well as the pride that the residents take in their homes, streets, and neighborhoods.

David T. Lewis
David J. Boehlke

NEIGHBORHOOD:
A STATE OF MIND

MAN-MADE CITY
CITY-MADE MAN

The geography of Baltimore is not very broken up, it's all pretty much of one unit. But if any section can be said to stand out, it has to be East Baltimore. This is the only one where, when you write it for a newspaper, putting it in print, you capitalize the direction of the geography. *East* is uppercased, capital letters.

East Baltimore, and all other sections of town, are famous for their row fronts. People's eye is caught by the marble steps, and the marble comes from quarries way up north of the city. But the bricks, in good part, come from East Baltimore. And there are firms over there now which still turn out billions of bricks. So it was no accident that East Baltimore had these endless vistas of bricks. *James H. Bready*

It was terrible. It was a door here and a door here and everything was blocked—you know—boxed in, everything. All the rooms were separate—everything was boxed in. So I started cryin' and my husband says, "Well, Estelle, don't cry. You like the street—we bought the street, we didn't buy the house. Let me fix it up and see what happens and then if you don't like it, we can sell it." I said, "Well, that way, all right." So I never forget it. Fronnie comes in. "Oh, what junk you bought. What's the matter? Where was your eyes?" I says, "Where were my eyes? In my head. But I didn't see the house. I bought the street. Don't you understand?" *Estelle Figinski*

Sure we had an outhouse, but we only had a two-holer. Our rich neighbors had three-holers. *Selma Katzenberg*

Beautiful! Beautiful! [The garden] used to have these here hollyhocks, used to have these here rosebushes on top of rosebushes, small plants,

used to have little cedar trees. Oh, it was beautiful. Lady next-door had the same. Lady next-door had the same on both sides....Old wooden fences. The neighbors used to whitewash them in the spring of the year, and they used to stay until the fall of the year. *Frederick Hirschman*

Mrs. Hirschman and I have been working together...as far as our yards are concerned. She decorates her yard at Christmas and Easter the same as us. And Labor Day, Memorial Day, Fourth of July, we have flags all over the yard.... There have been people who have come up and took pictures of it....And people that I've met said they never saw anything like that in the city. They just can't get over decorating the yards, but we get a kick out of it. *Anna Goddard*

I have always decorated the window. Started on Christmas, as a matter of fact. We had a beautiful Christmas tree, but my boy said, "Well, Mom, nobody can see it. Why don't you put it in the window where everybody can see it?" And that's the way it started. I never realized how much pleasure other people are getting out of it. The grown-ups will come real close to the window, and they'll look and say, "Oh, my, isn't that beautiful." And the little children with my basement windows, I always had that fixed for the little children...and they just love it too. And they all say, "I don't know who lives there, but that window is always so pretty!" *Mary Ordakowski*

In East Baltimore you want things paved solid. One reason is because it's easier to clean. The mentality that washes the marble stoop also sweeps the sidewalk. And trees out there drop things. The dogs that come along....All over Baltimore they were trying to get trees planted.

But in East Baltimore they kept saying, "Don't plant trees here in front of my house."
James H. Bready

My grandfather would take me around to the stockyards sometimes, and that was really fun. We'd watch the pigs come out the ramp. Course that may not sound fun, to you, they stunk, but when you're a kid, and the only thing you know is paved sidewalks and you've never seen a pig before in your whole life or been around a farm, it was an experience. *Betty Deacon*

In them days they, Schluderberg [Esskay, in Highlandtown] ran a slaughterhouse....They used to drive, take all them cows and lead them right up that street, cobblestones. Just like they do in the west. *Adam Glowacki*

We used to have all the factories down here: Standard Oil Company, the copper works, fertilizer factories, and we had all kinds of canning factories. In fact, when anybody came near Canton, they knew where Canton was. They could smell it. *Isaac Highstein*

My father had a stall down Canton Market.... He had a produce stall down there....There was lots of stalls in the Canton Market. Different produce stalls, different fruit stalls. There were butchers down there that sold meat. There was also people that had milkshakes and snowballs, ice cream...,Well, it's been a number of years now that that market's been torn down.
    You rented a stall....It wasn't closed in. You could walk into the market from any side, but each stall was separated, and the stalls were like a big table, closed in the front but open in the back....My father could decorate his stall right nicely and neatly....I know when he or

my oldest brother loaded their wagons to go out, they were very attractive...with all different kind of fruit. They would pack boxes on the bottom of the wagon and then set boxes on top of that to display their fruit and produce. Sometime they put something under them to put them on a slant. They would hang a big bunch of grapes around on their wagon just to let people see what they had....My father also sold rabbits...and every Friday night as we were growing up, my father would kill chickens....They were fresh-killed chickens that my people sold. *Anna Goddard*

Butchers Hill? Well, I'll tell you. Up to the First World War it was mostly inhabited by rich merchants. Their families got big, thinned out, died, and so forth. Then the Jewish people started to move in, the rich ones. And they would keep it beautiful, too. Then, just prior to the Second World War, again what happened was that families got bigger and thinned out. And there was a shortage of space for the migrant workers coming in for the industries. So they started renting them out. And they went to Florida, they were absentee landlords, and then started the down decaying point of this area. *Casimir Pelczynski*

So you had a lot of Appalachian people who had arrived, and Baltimore City was too big for them to get a hold of. But if they landed in East Baltimore, then they could figure out how to manage, because you can make a neighborhood of six blocks in East Baltimore, and you don't have to go out of that neighborhood. You had a sort of area that you could call your own turf. You knew where it was, you didn't have to get lost. *Mary Bready*

In East Baltimore you had everything. You had the clothing factories, such as my dad's, and you had the barber. You had the baker, and you had the dairy store, and you had everything. You had the shoemaker, and what didn't you have? *Sam Moss*

This particular part of the city [Fells Point] was "sailor town," and most of the bars catered to seamen. At the same time it was an ethnic area. You had a mixture of all people—Polish, German, Irish, and Spanish, and we all worked together and lived together. *Helen Christopher*

I remember the pagoda at Patterson Park which was very dear. You could climb up there and be able to see the whole part of East Baltimore, even down to the waterfront. *Rose Rodner*

July the fourth, Patterson Park became the fireworks center of the city of Baltimore. *Sam Moss*

It was the packing houses, the likes of people working, that built the beautiful Polish churches that enhanced southeast Baltimore. *John M. Mengele*

Of course, what we have most of are churches and bars. We don't know whether the bars came in first and the people started feeling guilty and they built churches, or the churches came in first and the people started feeling guilty and went to the bars. *Father Lou Esposito*

View of East Baltimore taken from the roof of the old
National Brewing Company building in Canton.

View of East Baltimore looking west. Brick row houses and white marble steps symbolize
these working neighborhoods. White marble steps represented a note of elegance and a mark of
respectability to newly arriving European immigrants. Keeping them clean became an art.

Ann Benvenga's window, Highlandtown. On a street of otherwise similar row homes
the front window often shows a degree of individuality and is sometimes used as a showplace
for its owners' creativity. Often gifts and cards are displayed for neighbors to view.

Anthony's, owned and operated by John and Mary Zadroga, is one of the few remaining sidewalk markets in the city of Baltimore. Mr. Zadroga's father started the business on Eastern Avenue in 1946, and John has been managing it since 1958. The Zadrogas live above the market. They have three children, none of whom plans to come into the business.

The Arab wagons are no longer loaded from this stable on Aliceanna Street
in Fells Point. The building has been purchased by H & S Bakery.

Hebrew Friendship Cemetery, founded in 1847.

Butchers Hill is one East Baltimore neighborhood whose identity has continually changed. By the mid-1920s most of the butchers had moved away and were replaced by Jewish doctors, dentists, rabbis, grocers, confectioners, and barbers. After the Second World War, many of the Jewish residents began migrating to the suburbs. The larger homes were converted to apartments. Neighborhood identity dissolved and the quality of life deteriorated.

Houses were built in close proximity to the packing houses
and canneries at the turn of the century.

Backyards, Highlandtown.

View of East Baltimore looking north.

35

As itinerant screen painters have retired or died, painted window screens—a popular Baltimore art form—have gradually been disappearing from the windows of East Baltimore homes.

In East Baltimore, backyards and alleys are an extension of the living space of the family
and are, therefore, maintained with the same care as the interiors of their homes.

A HERITAGE TO SHARE

Well, I think that the people from Highland-town could teach the rest of Baltimore how to live with respect to the way they take care of their homes, the way they save money, the respect the children have for their parents, the way they get along together.
Judge Carl Bacharach

People identify themselves by parishes. "I'm from St. Stanislaus," "I'm from Sacred Heart," "I'm from Pompei" —or St. Brigid's or St. Elizabeth's or St. Wenceslaus. And many times it's a rather embarrassing situation because you might be talking to someone who happens to be Protestant and they say, "What's a Pompei?"
Father Lou Esposito

In this house, we've been here since '41. When I bought this house, I'll tell ya, it was meant for me. I saw an ad in the paper for this house, and I says to my husband, Walter, "That would be just nice for us. I like this neighborhood." He said, "All right, we'd go to see it tomorrow and see." Well, I was more religious than I am to-day, I don't know why. And I says, "Blessed Mother, if that house is supposed to be ours, give me some kind of a sign. And I would like for it to rain, then I can't take my son to kinder-garten, then I'll go look at the house." Sure enough, I got up Monday, it was raining. I says to my husband, "Let's go get the house because it's raining today, and I know the Blessed Mother wants us to buy that house."
Estelle Figinski

Really we had very little material things, but there was so much pleasantness in the neigh-borhood. The neighbors were really and truly neighbors, good neighbors. We exchanged foods, different types of foods. And we visited one another in our homes and all the children. There were just no differences. *Rose Moss*

The mothers or the daughters would wash the marble steps in the afternoon, and then toward evening you would see, here and there, down the whole block, the white patent-leather shoes or the new gingham dress that the mother would get. And the ice cream man with his pushcart would come up, and you would sit on each other's steps. *Sam Moss*

When we were children, this was peaceful, like the country. You could put a blanket out here on the pavement, it was so clean. And all the neighbor children would sleep out there all night and never be disturbed.
Johnny Eck

I'm speaking about my neighbors....The lady [next-door neighbor]...we have a pathway, we call that an alley. Well, I haven't been in her house at all but twice since I'm livin' here, and I'm livin' here forty years...because I know her husband didn't like nobody to come in....We talk outside, we all get out in the summertime. We all sit outside, and we talk to one another, but don't have the habit runnin' to one another's houses. That's not our habit. If something would happen, like an accident or something....Oh yeah, we'd run over there...but like this, we don't go to nobody's house around here. We sit outside, we see one another. Why [would] we want to run in to one another's house? In cold weather it's very sad because we don't see nobody unless we come out. We don't bump into one another or unless we wash our step or wash the window.... Then when we see one washing the step, then we go out to wash it so we can talk to the neighbor. And that's the way we see one another in wintertime. *Estelle Figinski*

We have a beautiful alley. We paid to have that alley cemented. It cost me fifty-three dollars. And now the kids come here to play ball. One time I says to him, "Louie, what are you playing ball here for? Go on your own alley 'cause you're gonna break a window. Who's going to pay for it?" He said, "My mother told me to play here 'cause our alley is too dirty. It's too much dog mess...." One day the boy came down the alley with a dog, and I said to him, "He messed. Look, you pick up that dog mess or I'll get the police." So, he went home and did it. He told his father, and the next day his father came down and, for spite, let the dog mess. The man down the street told him to pick it up, and he wouldn't do it. I said, "Okay, I'm going to call the police." Finally, he did pick it up. But they moved. They said they couldn't live in a neighborhood like this because they said it was too strict. *Mary Kujawa*

It was, unfortunately, sort of natural when East Baltimore, in the 1950s, deserted the brick look and put up a thing which in the trade name was called Formstone. You gotta remember your East Baltimore homeowner is pragmatic. He or she was sold on that for something that had nothing to do with appearance. I suppose that they told 'em that it would keep them from having to have the bricks painted, or that it would make the house less leakable.
James H. Bready

I was fortunate enough to represent a building and loan association in East Baltimore, and it was basically an Italian-Polish neighborhood. I was there every Saturday night for seventeen years. They came in with their children, taught them how to save. Every kid in the family had an account. Some part of the weekly wages went to savings. If there was a wedding, there was always money in the building and loan to pay for the wedding. No matter what they made, some part of it religiously was deposited each week. *Judge Carl Bacharach*

If they owed you, if they came in and an article was ten dollars and she had five, she would say, "I pay, I pay." "Well, I don't know your name." "It's all right, I pay." That's what you would hear. And as soon as sun came out tomorrow, they would be there, and they'd pay. I have never lost one dollar on one Polish family, not one dollar, until this day, and you know it's some forty years I'm there. *Dora Schwartz*

You always made yourself a few cents. Nobody went to welfare. Because these were Polish people, you know. We were independent. We don't want nothing for nothing. We want to work for it. *Julie Zack*

And the other thing which is very beautiful in our neighborhood: I believe we still have mostly interpersonal relationships, rather than interfunctional relationships. Everybody knows everybody. The children grow up together, they come to school together, and as a consequence it is a close community in a sense, with all the faults and the good points of a close community. *Father Lou Esposito*

I went to St. Casimir's School for eight years which was...very strict, and they taught me how to speak proper English, with a ruler.
Maria Celluzzi

I wasn't much on learning anyway. I might not have the education, but God gave me other things I can do. That I can knit, I can sew, I can crochet, I can do most anything. I can do my ceramics very well. So, I'm fortunate that way. *Estelle Figinski*

I went to St. Casimir's School. Everyday, before school started, we had mass. It was one of the nicest parts. It did give you a lift. *Jo Anne Sanders*

The only problem with going to that school is that the priests were so strict that you had to go to mass everyday and have communion everyday. For little kids I didn't understand that. It got to the point that really I had a very...I didn't have anything to confess, and I had to make up lies to confess things. *Maria Celluzzi*

I went to St. Stanislaus School to the eighth grade. Forty-two children in each grade. Now they're lucky if they've got twenty. I graduated from St. Stanislaus, I got married in St. Stanislaus, buried my husband in St. Stanislaus, buried my mother in St. Stanislaus, buried my father in St. Stanislaus. My daughter graduated from St. Stanislaus, my son graduated from St. Stanislaus, and he got married there. *Julie Zack*

I had a baptism. Five generations were present. I had the girl, the mother, the grandmother, the great-grandmother, and the great-great-grandmother. They all live within a block of each other. *Father Lou Esposito*

In fact, my grandmother was ninety-one when she died, and I had her home with me. Now I have my eighty-one-year-old father home with me. Of course, I guess you know that people in this neighborhood don't believe in age towns, or senior citizen towns. They just believe in keeping your parents with you and taking care of them. Do for them what you want done for yourself in later years. *Veronica Conley*

Well, when you're born and raised in a neighborhood, it seems like that's where you want to stay. You know, that's the way I feel. I'm going to stay here until I die. *Mrs. Francis Lukowski*

My father never ever let go of his ties in Italy, and he instilled that in us. And he never ever lost track of anyone in his family. My mother, the same way. He always used to say, "The United States I love. Italy I love, but Italy I love like my mother. United States I love like my mother-in-law." *Josephine Vacca*

They like everybody to know what their nationality is. So, most of them will identify themselves first as Italian, German, or...and then they say, "Look, I am an American." They will add that very quickly, but first they will say, "I am an Italian," "I am a German."
Father Lou Esposito

My father came from Lithuania, my mother came from Poland. He got a job down the can shop on Wolfe and Aliceanna streets. My father used to come home for dinner 'cause we lived at 1904 Bank Street near Wolfe Street. There was a bar 'cross the street with a swinging door, and the bar was owned by German people, which they still are in existence there....I would look underneath the door and I would say, "Hey, Mister, my father wants some beer in his kittle"....He would say, "All right." He would fill the kittle up, which I paid ten cents, and my father would have his beer with his dinner.

My father was very good on buying United States bonds. He would buy one every time they would come around. He took his first American citizenship papers but he didn't take his second, but he was a better American than some who are born in this country. *Estelle Figinski*

Back in the late '40s, there was great competition between the Italians and the Poles. God help the pretty little Italian girl who danced with a Polish boy in Patterson Park at the casino because this was enough to start a real riot in the park.

The park pavilion, which was a large sort of open-air thing with windows all around it, and a stage, and a place for music, was a dance center. We used to check the kids in, as they came in, and we used to check their brass knuckles, quite—I mean this was automatic. You took their coat, their hat, and their brass knuckles as they came in, and when they left you gave them their coat, their hat, and their brass knuckles, and they went out and beat each other up out on the brick pavement on the way outside. If you had taken in a great many brass knuckles in the course of the evening, you tried to get a call in to the park police before you gave them back out at the end of the evening. *Mary Bready*

This is a very prejudiced neighborhood. I'm certain you're all aware of it. They wouldn't accept blacks rather well at all. Many reasons, I guess, we used to go through the same problems. The Italians, the Germans, and the Irish have made it, and they don't want to be reminded of their conditions only a couple of generations ago. *Father Lou Esposito*

I remember walking up Regester Street. Children around there, Irish or Scottish or somethin' like that, was throwin' stones at us and said, "We don't want you Bohunks around here."...People were prejudiced against my ethnic background. When I was a little kid, I couldn't understand how these kids and people over there are throwin' stones at us and stuff like that. To me, I don't care what your color is...until you do somethin' bad against me...you're a person to me like any other person. Treat me right, I'll treat you right. *Casimir Pelczynski*

I say I really enjoy it here with all the people. I go to St. Brigid's to a luncheon, St. Casimir's to a luncheon with the ladies. I belong there to a Sodality of St. Casimir's, we belong here to Sacred Heart. I belong to the Holy Family and the Ladies of Charity. We go to parties and I make things for the bazaar. And that's the way we live here. But, this is the most wonderful place to live for anybody's thinking. *Mary Kujawa*

I play at least two nights a week at different churches where the prize money is best. I think I'm going to go out of my mind during Holy Week without bingo. *Albina Kinder*

The Fourth of July celebration started twenty-three years ago in two yards....On the Fourth of July morning we get up at 6:00, we clean the yards and the alley and then we start decorating. At one time we had four hundred flags up the back alley....For twenty-three years there has never been one argument at all in the whole block party. *Alvina Marski*

In the early days when death visited a family like it did when great-grandmother passed away, a crepe adorned the front door, telling passersby that someone had departed the earthly confines. Around grandmother's coffin was profusely adorned with many, many roses. *John M. Mengele*

And voting time, most politicians hit the bars. Because at that time a bar-owner could swing a lot of votes just by talking to his customers. *Helen Christopher*

My campaign [for Democratic State Central Committee]...mine was really the raggle-taggle armies of the poor, believe me. My publicity signs were made by retired nuns of Mount St. Agnes. One of my friends in the neighborhood...hand-cut press-on black-eyed susans and daisies. They were my campaign flowers with "Vote for Gloria Aull" out of plastic. And I carried a huge bag of lollipops over my shoulder, and I gave lollipops out to all the kids where I went. And my official campaign car was a Volkswagen convertible which belonged to two friends of mine. And I had plastic roses because poor people can't pay for real roses. *Gloria Aull*

But ours was really a life of plenty—plenty of relatives, plenty of neighbors, holidays, cats, fights, parties, illnesses, weddings, and superstitions. Although many times we could only afford second-class merchandise, because of Mama and Papa's guidance and love, we were first-class citizens. *Rose Moss*

A Canton homeowner maintaining East Baltimore's reputation for clean sidewalks.

Mary Kujawa in the doorway of her Canton home.

The Taylor family, Butchers Hill.

Marie and Grace, neighbors in a Butchers Hill row house converted to apartments.

Solomon Faiman, eighty-five years old, sitting outside his new-and-used clothing store, which
he has operated for sixty-five years at the same location on Lombard Street.

Gathering in Canton to watch the relocation of the roof from the
historic Canton Market to the new Ellwood Park Playground.

Nan Cotrelle Coiffeurs, in Canton, a few days before Easter.

Fund-raising fashion show for the benefit of St. Stanislaus
Kostka Church hall, damaged by fire.

Eating Together—more than a hot meal at noon.

Nuns at the gaming table during the Polish festival in Fells Point.

Preparing the annual sauerbraten and dumplings dinner
at the United Evangelical Church, Canton.

Mr. Kolarik, a weekly shopper at the Linwood Bakery, in Highlandtown.

Doris and James Williams in their Butchers Hill grocery store. Friends and neighbors
stop by each morning for coffee and to catch up on the news.

Hochrein's Bar.

Afternoon break, St. Elizabeth's School.

The neighborhoods of East Baltimore are still predominantly Catholic, and each church reflects the ethnic heritage of its parishioners. Melissa Massaroni lives in the Italian neighborhood of Highlandtown. She has just taken her first communion at Our Lady of Pompei Church.

Elizabeth's memories.

Detail in a two-hundred-year-old home in Fells Point.

Rose Comi with nieces and nephew, Renée, Trish, and Bernie,
at a family New Year's party in Highlandtown.

Fronie's Christmas altar.

Funeral service for community leader at St. Michael's Church.

Parade in Patterson Park prior to St. Elizabeth's annual Palm Sunday balloon mass.

Pulaski Monument, Patterson Park

Polish East Baltimoreans have honored General Pulaski, one of our revolutionary war
heroes, by erecting a monument in Patterson Park. A commemorative service is held each October;
a band performs, speeches are made, and flowers are laid at the foot of the monument.

Boy Scouts guarding the symbolic tomb of Christ,
Greek Orthodox Good Friday service.

St. Anthony's Day Festival, Little Italy.

Albert Hoffman reading daily prayers at B'Nai Israel Shul, Lloyd Street.

All Souls Day procession at the St. Stanislaus Kostka Church cemetery.

Delores Conners at VFW hall in Canton on Memorial Day.

Polish-American war mothers on steps of St. Casimir's
Church on Memorial Day, 1979.

Choir of St. Matthews United Methodist Church.

The Eichenkranz group: Ray Strickroth, violin; Herman Grofebert, piano; Gerhardt Senula, guitar; and Walter Fellicht, mandolin.
They jokingly refer to themselves as the "Medicare Four" and the "Social Security Swingers."

Mr. and Mrs. Peter Frenchy on the occasion of reconfirming their
wedding vows on their fiftieth wedding anniversay.

The Marski family and neighbors at the annual Fourth of July celebration which began twenty-three years ago in two backyards in Highlandtown. Since then, it has expanded to include the entire block on both sides of the alley. In some years as many as four hundred American flags are flown.

LIVES OF WORK

In the old standards of America, plumes over smoke-stacks meant jobs for people.
James H. Bready

The packing houses was where all the people who didn't understand English worked. They knew what a penny was and what a nickel was, and that's what they got paid—a few pennies for a bucket of tomatoes. And in the late evening my mother used to come home, put her pennies and nickels on the table and count 'em. A lot of those pennies and nickels had tomato seeds on them, and they smelled so good, like Little Italy. *Frank Krajewski*

They used to have canneries [in Canton] that worked all year 'round. They packed pineapples and they packed peaches. They packed spinach, beans, sweet potatoes, and in the middle of the winter, they even packed oysters—steam 'em—and that's where most of our work came from. I shucked many an oyster myself, to help my sister out. My older sister, she used to be capable of steaming a hundred, a hundred twenty-five buckets—a good-sized bucket, probably at least a three-gallon bucket—in a day's time....Day meant to us, well, we never counted the hours. We used to start at 7:00 A.M., then you would have a little break for lunch, and then you'd work until the day's crop was harvested and packed. Never left anything go overnight.

We used to work in the canneries for about six weeks in the summer after we came back from the farms and after school hours. Why, we didn't go around and go to any drugstore or anything. We came home and took our one shirt off and hung it up nice. Took our one pair of shoes off, and then we went to the cannery.
Casimir Pelczynski

Summers, when we were small kids, my father used to take the whole family down to Anne Arundel County, where we lived in a shanty, and we'd sleep on straw with heavy canvas covers. We worked on a farm. We kids were the pickers and our father was a row boss. It was a hard job, but I tell ya, everybody was happy.

Well, my mother would get up about 4:00 in the morning, and she would have hot coffee for us. We would just wipe our eyes off with water, and we would drink coffee, and then we would go to the field. By that time it was a little lighter that you could see strawberries, but oh, was it cold. It was that dew, and it was so cold, it was wet, and when you were hungry, you were eating strawberries for breakfast. *Estelle Figinski*

The living conditions was what we made it. Now, one of the chores of the children, boys in particular, was to run and lay claim on one of the shanties. They were like quonset huts, and it was partitioned. The bigger the family, the more room they got. And the first thing all the men did, they had to get one stove up. You see, they used to make their own stove. They would take clay and water and straw and make the base and put a big metal plate over the top of it. Then the women could go around and start cooking coffee. The next thing they would concentrate on was the oven. It would take about two days to do that. Then all the men would pitch in, and everybody would get a stove. As far as bed was concerned, we had twelve-inch boards, then the whole area was filled with straw, and then sheets put on top of the straw. And we'd whitewash the inside of it.
Casimir Pelczynski

In the back of my house here, about three blocks down, is Esskay's plant,...which is a

German meat-packing plant. My grandfather worked there. My grandfather lived in this house. He was a meat wrapper there. My mother worked there. When she first started working, she was a sausage stuffer there and linker. [She] worked herself up to being one of the fastest linkers in the plant.

My grandmother was a barmaid at Shenning's Bar. But a barmaid in those days was different than what a barmaid is now. Shenning's Bar, that's where you stopped to cash your paycheck, okay, everyday. So my grandmother was kind of in charge of making sure that the men got out as soon as possible and home with their paycheck....She'd make sure they'd have no more than two beers, and then they had to go home. They could always come back later, but they had to go home and get their paycheck home. *Betty Deacon*

When I started working [Arabing], I was too poor to have a horse and wagon. I had what you call a "Hoover Cart." It was a baby carriage. You would put a fish box on a baby carriage, lay it on there, and you were in business. I am making one now, and I'm going to put a big sign up on it: "Hoover Cart in Carter Time." Did you get that? Ain't Carter the president? Hoover was the president then.
Paul W. Watkins, "Hots"

There were eight children in our family. My father was a tailor, and everyone of us was weaned on a sewing machine. *Sophie Nardone*

I was sixteen when I went to work at the cigar factory....My first job was learning how to roll cigars, and I was paid five dollars a week for learning....I was a very fast roller; I could roll about seven hundred fifty cigars a day.
Sophie Rominski

I taught buttonhole-making, would you believe it, a graduate of the Maryland Institute....I had the distinction of teaching Polish girls, Italian girls, Lithuanian girls, how to make a hand buttonhole....They didn't come into the shop....At sixteen years of age, I had the distinction of delivering work to the houses. So you had to take a big bag of vests to the house. Next day you picked them up as you brought them again. *Sam Moss*

I had two uncles who were barbers, so my brother and I got into barbering—they put us into it. I was a lather boy,...and I learned how to shine cuspidors—that's spittoons, if you want to know—them days they used to chew tobacco and spit in cuspidors. So we had to learn from there on, keep the floor and shop clean.

Then we would start lathering beards, then we would start shaving, then necks, and then we'd start on cutting hair. So that went on, and later on I became a barber. My mother had a shop near Fells Point, and my brother and I used to run it....We used to work belated hours, especially Saturday night....We'd be between one and two o'clock Saturday night, ...that's our business. *Adam Glowacki*

I was trained by one of my uncles to do shoe repairs. I started when I was about six years old. I started by picking up nails on the floor.
Paul Musotto

And the hours [in the store] were terrible. I mean, you'd get up to open 6:00 in the morning, stay 'til 10:00 at night, seven days a week. And, well, people didn't want to be on relief. It wasn't the idea of making a lot of money, because you could never make a lot of money. But it was just the idea that you wouldn't have

to depend on anybody, depend on charity. That was the worst thing for people in those days. They'd do anything just as long as they didn't have to ask for charity.
Isaac Highstein

But that was like going to school for me. I only went to the fifth grade in school, but the dime store taught me a lot. I met all kinds of people. I had to make sure that I could spell the things that I had to order, and if I couldn't I looked at the box and made sure that I spelled the words right. It helped me with a little arithmetic because I had to know. *Martha Lane*

At the time we started the union down there I was president of the union. We wanted to buy Mr. Wey out. Just the employees pitch in enough money to buy him. We stuck together that much. It was such a family affair. All these people working all those years at such a small wage in comparison to the other industries around. We were pretty well off as far as feeding ourselves and families. It was a steady group. All good workers, too.
Eugene Nardone

And I had Kevin. . . . From the time he was two weeks old, he used to be brought up to the shop every day, and he was raised here, and he knew the business. When he was nine years old, he started getting paid for working—like sweeping the floor and such. He was very interested in the business, and when he graduated from college, we felt maybe he wanted to go out on his own, do something else, but he still wanted to stay here, and he took over, and now he's considered one of the master craftsmen in the granite business as well as marble. *Veronica Conley*

If I could get someone who would be more reliable, I would let him take over the business and eventually sell it to him. I'd like to see a young person get ahead and keep on. A bakery is really needed here, and we are one of the dying trades. We are really one of the dying trades. *Frank Krajewski*

I have been with the company for sixty years, and I come to the office every day. I have turned the business over to my son as manager and owner. I have been asked when I am retiring; I do not want to retire. This spring my grandson is coming into the business with me. That makes three generations of Hughes family in the ship chandlery business.
Charles Hughes, Sr.

Adam Glowacki in the barbershop that he has operated for more than fifty years. The shop occupies the former living room of his in-laws' home on "The Avenue."

Paul Musatto surrounded by some of the neighborhood children who come to
his shop to confide in him. He has operated this shoe repair shop for forty-eight
years, taking enormous pride in the quality of his craftsmanship.

Stanley Adams, broom-maker at the Atlantic Southwestern
Broom Company for thirty-nine years.

Joe Poodles in the pool hall which he has operated for more than fifty years. He is
active in the Boxer's Hall of Fame. He is a former boxer, the father of a nationally ranked boxer,
and has been given much recognition for his contributions to the boxing profession.

Charles Hughes, Sr., and Charles Hughes, Jr., owners of Vane Brothers,
the only remaining waterfront ship chandlery.

The harbor has always played an important role in the lives of the residents of East Baltimore. It was the landing
point for many European immigrants during the late nineteenth and early twentieth centuries. As one of the largest seaports
on the east coast it still provides jobs, fishing, and recreation for the many descendants of the early residents.

In 1975 the National Brewing Company was merged with Carling Brewing Company. Shortly thereafter the plant at Conkling and Dillon Streets was closed. As a result, most of the employees were either transferred or laid off. Five, including Herman Fischer, are still working in East Baltimore as plant custodians.

Paul Watkins has been the stable boss for over thirty years at a Fells Point livery stable. The building has changed very little since it was built in 1833. At one time over forty-five horses and wagons were kept here. They were rented to "Arabs"—fruit and vegetable vendors and "junkies" (junk men). The building which houses the stable was recently sold to a large east coast bakery. The last six horses were sold in early 1980. The stable is now closed.

Chris's Carry Out.

Young hucksters on Bank Street.

"Doc" Price's pharmacy in Canton.

Albert Vogt was born in Germany in 1900 and came to America in 1924. He
has been a practicing barber for sixty-five years. The barbershop that he purchased
in 1954 has served the Highlandtown residents for more than eighty years.

Frank and Helen Krajewski, owners of the Linwood Bakery, did all of their own baking for twenty-two years. Frank began his baking career at age twelve in his parents' bakery. The Linwood Bakery closed in the spring of 1980, shortly after Frank had a heart attack.

Stella Foods, owned and operated by the Kostis family for twenty-one years, features the finest quality imported foods, wines, homemade Italian breads, and Greek pastries in Highlandtown.

Irene Lawton has worked on the assembly line at the American Can Company for thirty-two years.

St. Patrick's Day at the Irish Pub, Highlandtown.

T. G. Tochterman and Sons, Inc., was founded in 1916 when Thomas and Anna Tochterman opened a confectionery store on Eastern Avenue. Mr. Tochterman also worked full time for a wholesale fish market. Seeing the need to bring bait closer to the fishermen, he began to stock peelers (crabs that have shed their shells) as bait. They added other fishing needs, and soon they had a full line of piscatory equipment. They are now the largest bait and tackle shop in the Baltimore area. Today, Tommy and Tony, grandsons of the founder, manage the business with support from their father and uncle.

Raul and Rosemary Marconi in their Italian import shop, Italia Canta.

Edith Massey.

Second Time Around is owned and operated by sisters Helen and Sylvia Phillips.
Members of their family show their support by passing along items that they no longer
want or need. The sisters rarely have to purchase stock for their shop.

Dr. Andrew Kunkowski graduated from medical school in 1922 and opened his practice on Eastern Avenue.
Some fifty-eight years later, he continues to see patients four days each week.

Father Nicholai, pastor of a Russian Orthodox church
which was formerly an Orthodox synagogue.

OUR STORIES
OUR FACES

My father never allowed me to speak English at home. But he wanted us children to learn two languages. So we were always spoken to in Italian. And it fared us well because each of us is bilingual now.

I wasn't four yet. I can remember being out in the backyard and saying to my father, "We are out of the house now. Do I speak English or Italian?" He said to me, "You see this fence all the way around the yard? That is still our property. You're still inside our property. Here you will speak Italian." *Josephine Vacca*

No one had to tell us stories or fairy tales to interest us in food. . . . If an egg fell on the floor, Mama remarked, "Oh well, I'll bake a cake." She would run her thumb along the inside of an eggshell in order to scoop everything out. If a piece of candy fell on the floor, we picked it up, kissed it, and ate it. We counted our blessings, not the calories. *Rose Moss*

There was a place called "Walters" that all the girls during the lunch periods would go in for their delicious lemon meringue pies that you don't get any more, and the girls were getting bigger and fatter and fatter and bigger. *Rose Rodner*

When we went to St. Stanislaus School, our mother kept buying us beautiful nice ribbons from Bloom's on Broadway. The Sisters told us we can't wear those ribbons 'cause everybody can't afford ribbons. . . . So Sister put paper ribbons in our hair. The whole school had nice paper ribbons clipped to their hair. We'd come home and our mother says, "What's that paper doing in your hair?" I told her, "The whole school has 'em, Ma."

We had a little trouble with Beatrice . . . she was a very well-built girl 'n' she put on them high heels y'know, for school. Sister would send a letter to my mother saying that they're going to collect in school and buy her low-heel shoes. My mother sent a note back sayin,' "Gee, that's very nice, if you can put low heels on her, I'll pay for them." *Estelle Figinski*

We had a gang, Chester Street gang. Them days they had a Canton gang, Washington Street was the Washington Street gang, Ann Street gang, they had a Broadway gang. . . . That's how we traveled them days. . . . So we had five or six good friends of mine . . . and we used to walk downtown, get into mischief . . . tried to tantalize women . . . flirt with them. *Adam Glowacki*

I was no wilder than any other kid. . . . Didn't do nothing more or no less. One thing we used to do . . . during prohibition. . . . I was a kid just roaming around, and I saw a vacant house. So, like a curious kid, I saw a place where I could get in. . . . And I was exploring around, up on the top floors where they had these barrels of mash, down on the next floor, they had the still, and down on the bottom floor where they had the bottling works. I knew what it was after I saw it, yes. . . . There were a couple of vases. They were beautiful. They were laying up there on the mantle. I mean, the room was a shambles. So, I just took them along with me. I've still got one of them. I was probably about ten years old. They couldn't very well report that somebody broke in. *Casimir Pelczynski*

Now you take me . . . I have nothing, I never did. I don't have it now, and I don't ever expect to have it . . . and that way I have nothing to lose. So that is really the way I feel about life. Quite a few people come here and they say, "Don't you ever feel bad because of the shape you're in?" I look at them and say "No, why should I?" The one thing that I'm thankful for is that I've got a fairly good mind and I know how to use it....

One Christmas they put a show on for the children who were unfortunate at the church. We were very poor at that time, we still are...but it was in the wintertime and Rob was twelve years old, and he had on a pair of tennis shoes in the dead of winter because my mother couldn't afford regular shoes, and she told him not to let anyone see his feet and see how he was dressed. And they had a magician, a showman. He started to put on a magic show, and then he got to the point where he needed help, and he asked for a boy out of the audience to help him. All them crippled kids. None of them could get up and walk, and Rob gets up with his tennis shoes...so everyone could see him. Did he catch hell! And the show went on and Rob helped the magician...and he gave Rob fifty cents for his trouble helping him. Before the show was over, he took a big sheet of paper, and he tore pieces out of it, and all of a sudden, it turned into a beautiful lace tablecloth.... When he showed it, all the kids went wild. So he said that the first child that can come up here and get that, he can have it. Christ, the kids were reaching for their crutches and some of them were falling on the floor. And I crawled over the top of the whole damn bunch, and it was bedlam, got up to the table and grabbed that tablecloth, and the magician's eyes bulged. *Johnny Eck*

My husband came from a very religious family.... Rabbi Forschlanger was going to perform, when I became engaged...in Hebrew it is called "tanayim."...It is written like a marriage contract, and I didn't know anything about it.... It was really my mother and my sister-in-law, and my aunts and my cousins who baked and cooked everything, and we all went to Workman's Circle Hall.... We had a marvelous time. Then all of a sudden everybody had to sit down. The Rabbi started asking questions. And he said to me, "What are you giving to your husband as a wedding gift?" I told him, "I was giving him me, just me." And when I said that, he thought it was so great. I didn't know that...at the tanayim that you're supposed to break dishes. All of a sudden, he grabbed all the dishes on the table, and he started throwing them to the floor. This is supposed to bring happiness. And I, I don't, I still don't know whose dishes he broke. But I know that all the other people started throwing dishes, and before you knew it, everybody was throwing cups and saucers on the floor. And this is what tanayim is. So, I can only tell you that everybody ate, and it was just a great party, and I got a lot of pretty presents. *Rose Silverman Weiner*

Funny thing about that.... Back in the days when I had courted my Lottie, they used to sing a song, went something like this: "Take your girlie to the movies if you can't make love at home." Well, my wife lived just about a block and a half from the old Broadway movies. I used to take her to this Broadway movie and we used to set in the back—back row—hold hands, kiss about every fifteen seconds—and we spent many, many an evening that way at the old Broadway. *Joe Poodles*

At Christmastime we went Christmas caroling and twenty people showed up, which amazed me because everyone said, "Oh, you're kidding, we're not going to walk around and do that." We walked in all the bars and all these little stores, and it was really fun. We had ladies come out on the steps and cry, they thought it was so nice. But the most fun was the Solid Rock Gospel Church. The preacher wanted to keep us in there. He was preaching to us on how, no matter what time of day or night, if we need milk for our babies or food for our mothers, we could come in there and get it. *Cassandra Pelczynski*

I decorate his [Elvis Presley's] window for every holiday, put new flowers in, and fix his window up beautiful. People come around and take pictures and tell me it's so beautiful....I love him, and I respect him, and I always will. As long as I live, I'm going to have him in my heart. *Elizabeth Wozniak*

I always remember my grandmother as being somebody that didn't fit the role as most other women in this community....She belonged to a ladies' card club. They used to play poker and pinochle for penny-ante. I thought that was really neat. And their card club used to go to New York, and I remember she used to take a fifth of Canadian Club, which was a very expensive whiskey, to a neighborhood like this. And they'd bring back pictures of being in the Statue of Liberty, and to me, that was a different country, going places like that....The interesting kind of thing, I think, is what happens in families. My grandmother worked, and I felt she was kind of a progressive lady...but then my mother did actually the opposite. My mother didn't work, she spent her whole life in raising her two children. And that's it! I feel exactly the opposite. I kind of

feel that I'm following in my grandmother's footsteps....I don't have any daughters, so I can't watch what would happen to them. *Betty Deacon*

Marta Nadozirny, born in the Ukraine, immigrated to Baltimore twenty-
seven years ago and has not yet adopted the English language.

Summer afternoon, East Baltimore Street.

Friday morning, Fells Point.

Neighborhood boys by the Bankard-Gunther mansion, Butchers Hill. The mansion,
built in 1864, was originally the home of a well-to-do butcher who amassed his fortune
during the Civil War by selling his beef and pork products to the Union Army.

For several years this lonely-looking man had sat in his doorway almost daily. One day a
small dog was perched on his lap. A neighbor said that she had given the dog to the man to keep him company.
Neither the man nor the dog has been seen sitting in that doorway since then.

After the home in which she had lived for over fifty years had been
burglarized more than twenty times, Helen Taylor was forced to move to
a better-protected, government-subsidized apartment in Butchers Hill.

Johnny Eck.

"Hots" and Bobby.

Paul Baginski in the Fells Point home where he has lived for seventy-five years.

Solomon Faiman.

Bobby Halcup, unofficial mascot of the Fells Point Division of the Baltimore City Police Department. Bobby's fascination with police life led officers to present him with this custom-made uniform.

Theresa Lee Oxendine.

Murty, Ananta, and Santhi Hejeebu.

Alice and Junior.

Mary and Michael Kujawa raised five children in their two-and-a-half bedroom row house in Canton.
They take considerable pride in the maintenance of the alley at the rear of their home.

Erica Ann Scardina in her parents' bedroom.
She was born on her mother's birthday.

Josephine Krolicka Balakir, Theresa Krolicka Vain, Marie Krolicka Hosza, Veronica Krolicka Wojcik, and
Agnes Krolicka Silk in the Canton bar Agnes and her husband have owned for the past twenty years.

The four Pajtys sisters: Veronica "Fronie" Poturalski, Catherine "Kosh"
Glowacki, Estelle "Stella" Figinski, Albina "Beanie" Kinder.

Matilda and Joe Koval in their Patterson Park Avenue living room. Matilda used to spend her days crocheting by the window. After attending her first SECO meeting, she formed a block club and eventually became president of Community Taking Action and vice-president of Neighborhood Housing Services. Joe is an accomplished television repairman, ice skater, photographer, and boatsman. Matilda is famous for her whiskey sours and her chocolate chip cookies.

Mr. and Mrs. Peter Frenchy in their dining room.

Miss May.

Elizabeth's window dedicated to Elvis Presley.

CHANGES AND CHALLENGES

The only thing that's changed here in the neighborhood is the age of the people, that's all. *Alvina Marski*

Years ago, when I was younger, I was ashamed to tell somebody where I lived [Fells Point] because this was a dead end. All of a sudden it became historical. It was historical before. *Julie Zack*

The neighborhoods don't change, but the people do. *Frank Krajewski*

At the risk of oversimplifying things, I think that the neighborhood population is basically divided into three segments: one, newcomers like ourselves; secondly, the older residents, more or less senior citizens who have been here for a long time, maybe even born in the neighborhood, who may have wished to get out but economically could not do so. And then there's the other group, maybe a little more transient in nature, the ones, I guess, at the lower end of the economic scale, so to speak, who don't seem to care or have as much invested financially or emotionally in the neighborhood.

   And the older, more established element ...have seen what's going on in the neighborhood. Perhaps [they] don't like it, but they might be a bit more hopeful now that there seems to be some new blood coming back and some old, rundown vacant properties being improved. *Craig Russell*

I think that they are afraid now to trust some young people. Okay? And maybe they don't understand that not everyone here that has long hair and a mustache is out to get them. You know some of those people, in fact, most of them have very good educations, and they are in a position where they can help my grandmother and her contemporaries. I just wish that my grandmother could be a little more open minded. I think that their styles of living sometimes bother her too because of her religious beliefs and because some of them aren't married and "living in sin." *Renée Wollschlager*

There's thirteen widows living in this block which had lived here almost all their life. And there's only two or three young couples moving in now, eventually. But as the older people die out, well, the younger people are moving in....And it's sort of a family affair. They never have to put a sign out, for sale sign, because from one ear to the other, and the home is sold. You've never seen a for sale sign in this block. *Sophie Rominski*

If you moved up and out, that meant you moved to Dundalk or you moved to Essex, or you moved to Belair Road. And then you got yourself a nine-by-twelve lawn in front of your house that you got to mow every Saturday. And that was moving up and out. And your house cost maybe $5,000 more than a house here. But people couldn't afford more than that, but that's how they moved up. *Betty Deacon*

The neighbors have changed to this extent, which I think is not for the good but for the bad of it. We're getting a lot of these transients from other states. And they're not the best type, incidentally, and it seems like they live on top of each other. They're not very sanitary, they live, let's say, let's put it this way: when they get out of bed, a new group takes over, and they sleep in the bed, and they just ran a vicious circle where they have fourteen, fifteen people, strangers, all living in one house.

The I-83...is going to run somewhere along Boston Street. They have destroyed many homes that lies in its path. And a lot of these homes were owned by the Polish people, that they worked very hard for, and then the city came along and condemned those homes. How much did they pay them? I don't know. But it was not what they were really [worth]. Some of them died of a broken heart. *Eddie Rich Siekierski*

And it was really through being very obnoxious and rattling a lot of chains that we finally got some recognition. That in itself becomes very disheartening and distressing. Because it kind of changes everybody's vision of the American dream, of democracy and everybody being equal and everybody having a fair share and being able to be heard. *Gloria Aull*

People in this community are traditionalists to a certain extent. But I think they're also willing to change if they have information, if it's good information, and if they are part of the process of that change.

I became very involved in school number 215 because that's where my sons went....There was a real thing going on when they were going to tear down the school....That building represented a mainstay in the community. It's a beautiful building. I mean the hardwood floors in there were beautiful. It did need renovations as far as a new roof, the heating system was outdated. They could have renovated the building cheaper than it took to tear that building down, bus the kids somewhere else, and rebuild that whole building. However, because of the way the money was funded on a state level, the state did not pay to renovate buildings, the state

paid to build new buildings. Ergo, there was no choice in the community....

There was a great feeling against open space because it was against traditionalism of what a school building is....So we got the school system to loan us a bus and some parents went out and looked at the open-space schools instead of just standing around saying, "I don't want my kid in just one big room with 50,000 other kids...."And it was effective....It was a really neat process that went on because housewives who only had a high school education or less...really became involved in the educational process. And watching those women go through that, in watching the kind of self-worth they started feeling themselves, was just tremendous. *Betty Deacon*

You'd be surprised how many people come back. People move out, move out to the county, but they always come back. They miss it, they miss the closeness, they miss the convenience of the stores, and movies, and their friends, their family. *Jeanette Wolf*

We have a grocery store on the corner that opened three years ago. There was no store in the neighborhood at the time. And for older people that can't walk to chain stores or have transportation, it's good. When the weather is bad in the wintertime, we got snow and ice on the ground, he [Norman, the grocer] would see that his neighbors got their bread and milk delivered to their home. He also participates in anything that we have. He donates hot sausage and all the hot dogs up the alley [on the Fourth of July]. He has wonderful meat, fresh cut meat. And he's a wonderful man. As I always put it, chain stores are all right, but chain stores don't deliver in an emergency. *Alvina Marski*

I think we were both looking to make something of a commitment to a neighborhood. Perhaps the city lifestyle, more or less, conforms to our own. I think to the extent that we're involved in what's happening here, it's been rewarding. But, it's been a lot of tension adjusting to the neighborhood. *Craig Russell*

We have just a wide range of people, people who are in various kinds of media communications. We have lawyers, we have students, we have teachers, we have people who are really good at various kinds of crafts, and electricians, and, the really nice thing is, everybody, their main concern is just to make it a nice place to live. *Cassandra Pelczynski*

We had a meeting on Thursday night, and we were discussing some of the crime problems in the neighborhood and what could be done about them. One of the suggestions was the forming of an escort service or a neighborhood patrol of some sort. We were having a discussion about the pros and cons of this kind of activity and one of the ladies, the senior citizens, was describing how she waits until the third or fourth of the month to take her Social Security check to the bank because then the purse snatchers don't expect you to have a check. These old ladies, as she calls them, who take their checks to the bank on the first are just crazy because they're asking for trouble. Somebody in the back of the room commented in response that she should be angry about having to wait until the third or fourth to cash her Social Security check. She should be able to go when she wants to go. She should have the right to go whenever she wants to go. So, at that juncture in the conversation, I said, "Anna, wouldn't it please you to be able to call

my husband and ask him to walk you to the store or the bank?" Anna just stood up and turned around and looked at me and said, "What will people say if I called your husband? We'd have a different kind of problem to deal with then." She was just hysterical. She was kidding around, but she was serious. She's all of seventy years old, and she's concerned with what the neighbors are going to say if she calls my husband over to her house. *Chris Russell*

Well, it's changing, but everything is changing, everything is changing, so what are you going to do? *Mrs. Francis Lukowski*

I've never been successful in organizing my own block. I put myself in good company by comparing myself to Jesus, a prophet that is not known in his hometown. But my neighbors would rather have me scrub my steps than go to meetings and carry a briefcase. And if you look out here and there's not an organizing issue on the block…it's a good block. *Gloria Aull*

And it is a lot of changes. A lot of people have died in the neighborhood, and the homes were sold, and different people bought it. But it isn't like when the older people lived here, but of course we gotta get used to it—to the other people that [are] coming in the neighborhood…and they're keeping up the homes. That's what means a lot. That when you look outside you don't see the homes that's falling apart. And everybody tries to keep the houses up and keep it nice and clean around the neighborhood, and that's what makes you feel better. *Mary Kujawa*

Four generations of the Goddard family.

The Mary Dean family.

Bonnie and Claude Aracil renovating their newly purchased Victorian row house in Butchers Hill. This neighborhood was so named in the nineteenth century when residences were built close to businesses. Dozens of butchers were attracted to the area because of the ease with which livestock could be delivered there from farms east of Baltimore.

Bill Pencek and Bill Heil are among the growing numbers of professionals who are buying and restoring
homes in Butchers Hill. Because of their commitment to this house, every small detail is given special attention.
They have retained the original floor plan, walls, floors, shutters, molding, and stained-glass windows.
Great care has been given to the selection of new wall and floor coverings, paint, and chandeliers.

Vince Peranio and Dolores Deluxe in their beautifully landscaped garden in Fells Point. The flamingoes are a carry-over from Vince's work as a set designer for John Waters's films.

Ruby Lowe.

Neighbors often visit each other on their front steps—extensions of their living rooms. This entire block is now under renovation by private contractors and individual homeowners.

Before the ground-breaking ceremony for Santoni's Market.

Awards ceremony at Boy Scout camporee in Patterson Park.

Viewing the "I Am an American Day" parade, 1979.

Ribbon-cutting celebration for a group of section-eight houses on Duncan
Street, Butchers Hill. These homes were renovated through HUD, and the residents
(mostly elderly) make payments or pay rent according to their ability.

The "I Am an American Day" parade is one of the largest social and political events of the year. It is organized and sponsored by the residents of East Baltimore.

PHOTOGRAPHERS' CREDITS

Linda G. Rich:

pages
27, 32, 33, 34, 35, 44, 46, 47, 52, 54, 56, 57, 58,
60, 61, 68, 77, 86, 89, 95, 97, 109, 110, 111, 114, 115, 118,
120, 121, 124, 126, 128, 129, 134, 136, 141, 143.

Joan Clark Netherwood:

pages
26, 28, 29, 30, 31, 37, 50, 55, 59, 62, 64,
65, 66, 67, 74, 75, 76, 87, 88, 93, 94, 98, 99, 101,
102, 123, 127, 135, 137, 140, 144, 145.

Elinor B. Cahn:

pages
36, 45, 48, 49, 51, 53, 63, 69, 70, 71, 72, 73,
82, 83, 84, 85, 90, 91, 92, 96, 100, 103, 108, 112, 113,
116, 117, 119, 122, 125, 138, 139, 142.